MAD WORLD,

MAD KINGS,

Wave Books Seattle/New York

MAD COMPOSITION

Lisa Fishman

Published by Wave Books

www.wavepoetry.com

Copyright © 2020 by Lisa Fishman

All rights reserved

Wave Books titles are distributed to the trade by

Consortium Book Sales and Distribution

Phone: 800-283-3572 / SAN 631-760X

Library of Congress Cataloging-in-Publication Data

Names: Fishman, Lisa, 1966- author.

Title: Mad world, mad kings, mad composition / Lisa Fishman.

Description: First edition. | Seattle : Wave Books, [2020]

Identifiers: LCCN 2019038464 | ISBN 9781950268078 (hardcover)

   ISBN 9781950268061 (paperback)

Subjects: LCGFT: Poetry.

Classification: LCC PS3556.I814572 M33 2020 | DDC 811/.54—dc23

LC record available at https://lccn.loc.gov/2019038464

Designed by Crisis

Printed in the United States of America

9 8 7 6 5 4 3 2 1

First Edition

Wave Books 087

I.

III.

IV.

<u>Note</u>: In the pages that follow, the tilde ~ is used to indicate breaks between poems, some of which are titled. Indented asterisks indicate breaks within poems. Whether by title or by bracketed first line/phrase, all contents are listed.

I.

Truth-telling is possible, thought Laura Riding, so the poem does not need to happen. That is, poetry should not exist. Rather, language should speak truth in all ways. Not in a separate realm, a special form, called poetry. Poetry existing as a separate category prevents language from speaking truth outside of poetry. Her decision therefore: No more poems. Write a dictionary. Where is this dictionary? Florida?

~

not "using words"

a way of being in the world, not extracting something from it

an interaction

~

the Five Ways to jump

the seven breaths

one pair of longjohns

the wine dark sea

the problem of 2016

~

Spring goes down
writing does too
sludge and muck
& sleep destroyed by hysterical birds

Who needs to sing at 4 a.m.

Riding says not at all

~

Michael says the poem will speak
to an unknown addressee

the poem escapes what it means to say

the poem's being in the world

~

Anyone says a few things breathing into a lightbulb and of course and especially we cannot find the mushrooms enjoying each other under the trees. But a little bit of infra-red kaleidoscope, lost in Michigan or Nebraska, opens partly with a quiver which a word is, also called a kangaroo, because it jumped and someone said it—also known as yesterday, Lamar and Liz and lots of us with different names. What letter are you on?

~

How is every giant lunatic today? Drawing a picture the
eye opens. Eye draws,
      here you are, three trees
in the snow, little cone-shaped
shrubby trees slanted as
a border for a driveway—
neighbors. No more
neighbors.

One friend is writing
winter another
is pounding copper
and there are plans
and plans to march.

The bees are sleeping, another Michael reports.
We eat some things in the city where
he has no car but many
hives, two roommates
(self & Solveig)
and is 68.

I don't know how to assemble
it any more—the pages and
words. Where are the notebooks
Notebooks—who knows?
Where they are,

what they say. Can you
hold me in tensility?
Say words

    Says each word

    ~

That walk up the hill in the
dark, with no moon no stars
no phone no
so the ground was met
not stumbling but not
surely, in the crusty
lumpy snow, unevenly
deep.

Walking is one-footed

    ~

Hill comes up
under foot
is one way to say it

Say "I'm walking"
and it's something else

    ~

Each thing seen is upside down
Brain flips it, so we see it
"right side up"
Can you believe this
even while spinning

~

I love you they say without music
Now it's over where were you flower?
Time, rhyme.

Today is December

last line is X =

Today is December 1st 2016

Today is ____

X = Y

Death is = ____

X   Y

Today is Dec. 1, 2016

I did see that leaf.

Missing the play.

Then the election.

Today is

Death is

tumbling out in a rush

"self-harming"

story of life in a time

~

Night Skiing

at first in the junipers
hemlock & spruce

the poem needs more space
than at first

~

Full moon if I could see it
where we said we'd be
one fine birth
That in a letter

said a round lie
who won
time word orifice
a day before 50
go away sun &
come around a little more

~

The March King has horse's ears
The Queen of the Birds loves Tom Horne

"Mad time, mad kings, mad composition"
James read to me this morning

But I misremembered. It's <u>mad world, mad kings</u>, etc.

Many times a person repeats
"I Love Athletes" is a title I imagine
the arms could be said to be waking
the course of true love all around
how is everyone
related do you find
the plums succumbed
to curculio—sounds like a typeface, but it'd be
a rotten one

Now we are three women
Now the pre-morning changes to morning

How is everyone not striking?

How's the Emperor of Tartary
says the dog to the window

Eggs came in from the neighbor's & stuff must be made or go to waste

One cake in the springform pan later, where to resume

~

The dawn redwood's branches curve up
so the tree's arms are smiling—is that from the inside
ask and tell
name a spell
beginning with bucket
Water the tree when you plant it
That's exactly how she wrote her p̱'s
Lorine I mean, missing Ann
and my collected
Kyger, Mayröcker, Stevens
Some friends
got together on Saturday
but I was driving Holly to the ferry
Mr. Flyspeck in the universe
don't come back to anything
fell in the buttermilk
Sister, forgot your pants

~

Tree is
a beauty
a beau tree
a hummingbird
kept coming to
the porch eave
No blossoms, no feeder, but a yard full
of milkweed full of bees

The hummingbird looks like an insect, not a bird
with translucent-seeming wings
So what so what so what

Finding the pencil soft enough and dark, I covered up the skull fragment some-
one placed on the dresser probably after sweeping

And yesterday a mouse was discovered to have died at the bottom of the laundry
basket a long time ago—only fur & dust are left and the smell

Red maple out the east window
Hickory very green out the south
It isn't Stately, Buck Mulligan, or Paul
I wanted to know what he meant
by repeating state in stately
I was 11, wanting to know
what was censored

TATELY,

the oversized <u>S</u>, the giant comma, at least in my mind

What reading's remembering, and what's new

It seems July & August are here again, not at the same time but somehow together

~

Winter

Cut sumac again so the fir has light

*

Fall

The earwig was not <u>in</u> the Northern Spy—
it was in the crevice between apple-top and stem

    *

Summer

Bedbugs turned out to be bat bugs. Bat bugs are forced out of old houses' attics
in extreme heat. Bats abandon the attics because they're too hot, then the bat
bugs travel down through the walls into the house. Bat bugs are indistinguish-
able from bedbugs except through a microscope, which the Rock County Health
Department does not possess, or did not use, when I brought in my bug in a jar.

We threw away our beds and much else.

Climbed up the sides of the dumpster three days later and dragged the mat-
tresses back out.

    *

Spring

The book is not chronology. The book is a mess
"which became the research of where things go."

    *

No memory

copying out of Calvino
"The world must be read backward."

14

~

Cilento

Examine likewise . . . Whether there be a water above the sky? Besides, whether the earth is animated? And that every star in heaven hath a soul, angel, or intelligence, to animate or move it, &c

Robert Burton

At Velia the Eleatic School, not the Ecstatic School as I first mis-heard, was started by Parmenides walking on olives all over the paths down to the sea. Announcing PIT! each time he removed one from his mouth and put it in the sand, the baby ate thousands of olives. A person singing we heard floating from stone houses stacked in the twelfth century on top of each other and around each other, hugging the cliffs against the shore. Brenda wrote: "The lover enters the place / where we couldn't love our mother." I have been thinking about that a long time.

~

Swiftwriting

Between days that inch off into heaven, some paradox seems sadder—so dilated, hugely toothed, hardly-drawn into tempests. Is writing eating? Feeling handsome, find rising above Portia's head. Can't buy two bloody herrings, Christmas bathing takes sides. Hello farewell hey Charlie bring tomatoes, get today's old humming-bird-feeder by the garage again to sing. Shyly, have it sing a song. But maybe a happiness hears under heaven's wild heart to flee a ~~dear dear~~ different scene—it's true. Really oh please. Until home by other places see, see, no faking time—taste oranges; speak, person, child, say hello.

~

Swift 2

It acted cat-like or pressed into summer. Elegant handsome and nothing mattered.
Testing intentions for going anywhere Sincinatti Ostuni Ithaca Terza Galactica
Salem Istanbul Feeling all careful like premonitions.

~

You have a noon face ten times outside
We can where the sun holds new
What is the moon you are allowed to say—hi bye
heave/oh if you read the
paper you will
grieve and know why
are you thinking now
at the letter's edge
bent shadow at the laughed
bed

If is the key we said
if the poem hands
have if in them

If thou tremante

~

There were broken birds in the trigonometry, and a mud turtle in the road. Did you pick that flower? Yes, in time. On the avenue you followed through the Capitol, someone asked you for a brick. You did not say carry it with both hands.

~

I notice my heart seems to come up closer to the surface of my chest and to beat really hard and fast while the rest of my body seems to contract and exist less, because the racing heartbeat of my heart has become so loud and hard as to occupy the entire space formerly taken up by my body as if the rest of me has disappeared.

Nervous
polis

nervous system

A merica strikes again, ending as
Roman Empire.
1 Ratman try to walk, foot
over toe, on Dante
on Blitzen o darling
old vixen the twelfth
knight's counting angels
of plate
tectonics—thus
harm now
angles crabwise

~

Again no mother was
intuiting rest dream weather
reason loss Los Angeles Laos Louisiana
and thoroughly going where she weeps,
talk very frightening, actually talking you
call matter to error, measure
terror, eat ardor, by itself young
with mandate like tears. Something
takes women outside dearly
toward a lost message failure
to thrive.

~

Sweet Go Go Lime
Sweet Spring Grass

There are nine words and a triangle
somebody brought to school

Barbauld—Washing-Day
         On Education
Godwin—Enquiry Concerning Political Justice
Blake—There Is No Natural Religion a & b
MW—from A Vindication of the Rights of Woman

As if he is
turning everything into language
w/o losing fidelity to
raw thing

Is stalling then

precision
tell the truth

~

Swift 3

If I don't take realism to Paris in december. Yvette had kettles with invisible
insects touching hot energy. Toes, people's arms, i-lids, butts, orange fingernails,
airyhair, freckles, windchime arms, actual-hands, good toe—so are gardens
trans, is Ezekielle? Will harm lessen? Tomorrow goes on (k)nowing less of time
present and (a)ghast. Dog-nose clouds, deathly clouds, Insubstantial, Tornado,
Elephant ear, Green-gold, cloud of Lament, Resistance cloud, Nothing Cloud,
Knife-throwing cloud, winter's-tale, YOUR-FACE, excellent madam, tra la. Go
few. Or yes and yes let's. Feather open angel matter after guessing ending a song.
Inter-winter, wordsummer, you-forgot-fall, Eastern Bluebird summer spring,
Trees are friendly? not always america

~

Writing

Small wooden ladders hook onto the truck.
The child plays House On Fire
for the pleasure of making the siren sound
for the pleasure of unhooking ladders
& leaning them against the burning house.

The cousin-doll, a wooden peg,
races up the ladder on her peg body
to spray water with her no-hands, no-arms.

Also, there is no house
just the start of a wood project:
a paper shredder we call the house.

Often the cousin-doll gets lost
and the child both grieves and stores the grief.
The wooden peg appears
as randomly as disappears.

I see that the bark at the base of the hickory
has green in it and blue, and I remember
trying to write about that.

~

Sorting

Baskets are expensive but may be found at thrift shops. Crayons are cheap and last a long time, longer than markers which lose their tops. Crayons go in baskets, cars go in baskets, airplanes and Legos go in baskets. Eggs and asparagus too, I see from a photo of eggs and asparagus in a basket on the table this summer or last. J's favorite books are *Hutterites of Montana* and *Here Comes the Strikeout*, about Bobby who cannot hit the ball. When he calls himself Bobby we say he has an imaginary self, not an imaginary friend.

Learning to speak seems preceded by learning to sing. "Goose," he requests, as in *Mother* (the rhymes). Dancing surpasses singing: "Dance," he commands, holding his arms up and out, his face most serious then.

~

Storing

If sorrow is stored in the body
take the baby out of the crib—OBVIOUSLY—
when the baby cries.

Inch it along, alleviation of suffering.

~

Correction to Klee: the blossom is active

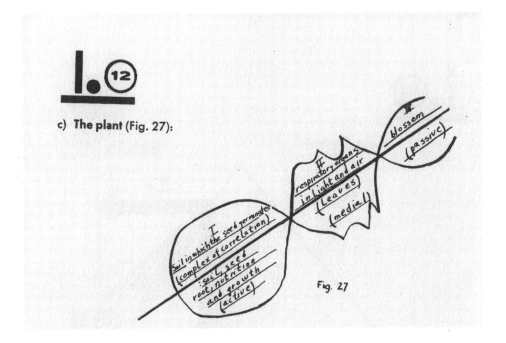

c) **The plant** (Fig. 27):

Fig. 27

~

"The sun's five hours slow"

"Ha ha! ha ha! Frightened . . . Timid!"

"He ran through the seeding blue-bells, and purple foxgloves, flowering under the nut trees and great oaks."

"He held his stick firmly and whistled softly as he walked warily, fearfully, on the soft moss."

"He ran down the stony path, where ants laboured among the patches of yellow pimpernel, under the roof of beech and elm, to the gate at the end of the wood."

The book was published five times between September 1931 and January 1944.

"Each animal takes his ashen twig and nails it over his door."

"THE END OF THE STORY"

Ha ha ha ha there is no world

~

Letter One: "It is a kind of rule at sea, not to send out a boat."

Letter Three: "Such are the effects of war, that it saps the vitals of even the neutral countries."

Letter Six: "My not understanding the language was an excellent pretext for dining alone."

Letter Ten: "They have a little patch of land about the distance of two English miles, where they make hay for the winter, which they bring home in a boat. . . . I suspect, by their furniture, that they smuggle a little."

Letter Thirteen: "You may think me too severe on commerce, but from the manner it is at present carried on, little can be advanced in favour of a pursuit that wears out the most sacred principles of humanity and rectitude."

Letter Thirteen: "It is not, in fact, surprising that the pine should often be undermined; it shoots its fibres in such an horizontal direction, merely on the surface on the earth, requiring only enough to cover those that cling to the crags. Nothing so proves to me, so clearly, that it is the air which principally nourishes trees and plants. . . ." (Mary Wollstonecraft)

~

Claw eth the cold at the throat / neck

Clothe it

what cost
    a short residence in
and the rights of

"a young woman, who is wet nurse to the mistress of the inn where I lodge, receives only twelve dollars a year, and pays ten for the nursing of her own child"

~

Worksheet, March 2013

quaking aspen grove it's called is
growing from a single

each aspen in the forest's from just one

so shadows tend the dense grown grove

get open yellow light

and yet

and then, and what

in making up the matted bed

of moss and loam and knot-twig down

says here am waiting for a known

outside of

English

into the forest went the men

messed up the weather

a woman

fishes out the lines and crosses out the missive

massive

swaths of gunk

cannot pry out a word the way some do

pry out the mammoth

tusks

ground in

the ground and buried in

I took

dictation from one age 3: WHOEVER WOULD JUMP AS HIGH AS THE SUN
                          WILL MELT LIKE WOOD IN FIRE

~

GUITAR   DRAW   STAR

the child says interchangeably and with some sadness

knowing we'll be momentarily confused

Wash my cap another said
as if to see how it sounded

I want something the woman said
not adding "beautiful" though it was added
by the listener

A box of small crayons for 39 cents
I found in the Orfordville Flea Market
Not a small box of crayons
but a box of <u>small crayons</u>: three inches long
Watching his eyes, I see it's greeted, not claimed

We've been hoping for a new president
though other things matter, not sure
at the moment how much

January 2007
Still hoping
for news of a candidate

~

Gulls lifted over
My Bestiary

The mothers floating
were sea otters nursing
under the clouds called mares' tails

Many animals stuck to the planet
the waves crashed up against
while you were talking

I wanted to take the child to a maze
because he likes to find his way through things

There was a maze of pumpkins
a maze of hedges and a maze of stones
very much to keep turning, and to love
necessitates another voice

I need to see where the river switches
from Level 3 to Level 4
if you expect me to get in that kayak

but really it isn't good enough
just seeing the pattern

~

A house has a cloud that's a rectangle over it (*agita*)
The roof is peaked (Saskatchewan)
The middle of the house won't fit, goes past
the frame of the house (*escribo*)
while the base of the house (bell)
is not a square. Off to
the side is
a window with no house

around it or maybe a
smaller house in the distance
(whorl).

~

Being asked to write the sounds. What is the sound?

Not a lion tamer in the riddle-dream.
Nor a cobra in my mind. Twelve knives
in twelve decks shine.

What did you think, the tongue is a fire?

~

What is the outside process?

SPACES btwn sentences!
Remember a scene of reading that was meaningful

or

A situation of disappointment—
something you wanted to happen that didn't

~

Memory Exercise

1 thing you saw <u>today</u>.
1 thing you heard <u>today</u>.

1 thing you saw yesterday.
1 thing you heard yesterday.

The day before yesterday: 1 thing you saw.
1 thing you heard.

~

When 10 voices appear
they're dizzy
[what they
say]
To speak is
to exist?

More are why
clear day was
what lost
speaking how
are you
good day

Why half a day, an ur-day,
dolphin, seeing you

gray skiing double
eyes, clearly you aren't
any half and the dolphin

You are why
clear day was
what lost
into thru
into la
speaking how

au revoir
what is departure
have you left your poetry
on the bus

~

transcription missing

destruction of nature

human

syntax?

~

Don't take apples from tortoise man?
I remember taking ribbon off a spool?
from a ribbon factory in Sweden?
The spool was wooden?
like a door?
and it was that shape, too?

~

Scraps

neck
& collarbone
ears
stomach
knees
eyebrows
wrists
fingers (+ nails)

~

The Fingers

are what seem to be both part of the body and potentially not.
The part that has the most life apart from the rest of the body.

~

I rode the Red Line longer than necessary last night?
It was the Purple Line first, then the Red?
The city was backward in the Loop?
"Woman, I know what that means?"
Persons and misery and fire and skin?

The day before yesterday is today?

~

D. H. Lawrence wrote a letter.
The penis points downward, he said:
A root cut off from the earth
needs to go farther down, not "UP"
to contact the ground it got severed from.

~

"While You Were Out"

*(On a pink message pad for telephone calls, use one sheet each time you write, walking around. Separate your pages with * when you type.)*

Daylight

*

28 seconds to cross the street

*

Pritzker Military Museum and Library
"holiday lights" in the shrubs (March 11)

    *

Clouds. A person's
breath coming out of her mouth.
My breath coming out of my mouth.

    *

4 landscape workers
2 in safety green
2 in safety orange
1 blowing leaves
2 trimming brush
1 carrying brush
and the lake farther out

    *

SunLight

    *

Some vertigo walking on bridge
writing while walking—bridge ends
up in the air

Godard-film-feeling
riding the escalator down

    *

up
some
stairs
behind the museum

"You are under surveillance"

    *

Thinking of evergreens

    *

Annella with a stick, making shapes or digging in the soft ground
Chainsaw work going on at home

    *

2 geese
2 more geese
Coming quite close.
Animals.

    *

We cross the street The sun is bright

The letters look like scribbling (hand is in a mitten)

    ~

Don Mee was talking
about the language of wound

she said flowers speak that language
enfolding geopolitics and poetry
more than one at a time

Tracie said her muse
told her to get lost
get lost in that form

~

I asterisk june like many months loving bad breathing asanas that make this
insufficient art bow wildly and after telling et cetera oh my love I owe a huge
other breaking.

~

Who was the? thing or one
question to open? the door
of a face? become hurt
as not listening? As woman, as worker
to disturb? I am the government
of an envelope? half-sealed,
I? and *you.*

~

What the Donkey Said

"We have had a most wrong vision"

Intentional error in the line
is the line—no not intentional—aware

the rocks rose
down to the sky

we have weather
it's the news

Did you bring vowels for the Frenchman
who'd know what silage is
if a man came in asking, "Oo eats the silage?"
on Sherkin Island

Later the forest came forward
dreamed and
she was that tree
stretching

The donkey woven out of everything
was the weaver sleeping
telling Moonshine, stand there
a round book named on the water
comes to the sentence again
Carla, Lotte, and Barbu

A strange thing today was the sparrow standing
on the edge of the drinking fountain, drinking water
in the airport—bending its head

to drink the water around the drain
but what
changes your mind
to a primary thing
a piece of grass
seemed stuck to the bird's toe claw
on the metal edge of the drinking machine
rough grass a field grass
the grasses part, setting you out
of the observed

Would you rather give up flying or driving
someone age 11 asks
speaking of ships
skateboards
drones

A stranger walks through the kitchen door
meaning to enter a different house
a bicycle should come riding through
and yes a pound of feathers
weighs the same as a pound of bricks
remember finding that
a magic fact

    *

Time and daylight
sleep in the tree, the noisy
inside of the tree

loud and more cacophonous
like the noise of many things
inside a shell, but more cacophonous
not really like sleep
or, how is that like sleep

The tree fell right out of its bark
it was in the redwoods but it was not a redwood
mere words in pencil

    *

a speck of sun fit between buildings today
while Henry picked apples & James being Ariel
found the printer's *ſs* as he'd hoped
in the second folio
Lotte went to upward bow
one leg at a time
from standing on her head

    —things at 4:30
on September 14th
in the midst of all the other things

    ~

November 16–December 1, 2016

another-
clatter-

calling-
for-
no-
public-
polis-
polar icecaps-

(or)

proud misogyny enters
double   double
pressing endless murderous
win   win

  *

battalions belted psychology
rigid lord hysteria
police central police

  *

Being completely fucked,
the song
rusts, rusts

Fathom fascism
hey-ho
chomp something

  *

president
joke
puke
bitter
joke

Pay extra,
mother

    *

bad bad lottery
marked everything marked final
country-america's terror-
ist vote

    *

bitterbreath
bentbreath
lockedbreath

clatterwinter
cut weather

    *

don't die don't die
aroundandaround
blue green blue green
waterwater
remember rem ember

＊

Beggars artists girls trans
literate sunk—persons places all.
How forage jack-bliss.
Fear comes without privacy or.

(or)

clanging clut-
ter out
throat
sphere
public
sphere
across
throat

＊

persons enter mashed
sun enter mashed
mind enter mashed
exit must exit

＊

but   but
broken held night
please remain re-
do cant, take all eloquence
from god's own mouth

*

Borne-out engine, stinging puzzle flung
past far outlying borders everybody says
everybody says, o failed mother mother
~~psst, opera's edges~~
please— ~~old English failures~~ become
ugly end, feel back, chime
present place please pass—
~~mirror chance~~
murderous chants ages ago

   [My pants are dirty but the couch is too.
   Mama is hungry. She will eat now.
   Mama's cheekbone juts out like a wave.]

and orphan excess fails
bent stuck left
hurt chidden
clatter message
  tug

   *

soundless - less - less
soundless - less - less
soundless - less - less

ash tree   ashtray   ashame

   ~

"i've been looking for you   i don't know why"

put everything in the present for the present
why would you think that
first line is a fiction
in the blizzard of '77
i was eleven

~

how far a person recedes
depends on the fox in the orchard
being seen and not made
into a hat
on the head of the neighbor
who walked past the window just under
the window, so the fox
was all you could see
bouncing by on his or her rump
because how the fox fits
on & around the neighbor's head
makes the fox appear to be bouncing
or scooting along
although it is dead, and its head
sits on top of the human's
& its body hangs down, split into two
to cover both
of the human's ears

II.

Wherefore she changed her mind

And he coupled five curtains by themselves, and six curtains by themselves

And she said Go

And he made loops of blue on one edge of one curtain from the selvedge in the coupling

And for the house he made windows of narrow lights

And the pots, and the shovels, and the basins

To the woman as she sat in the field

And she said Ships?

Three bowls made after the fashion of almonds in one branch, a knop and a flower

And three bowls made like almonds in another branch

Out of the place where she was

~

Da Vinci wrote, "If the sun is in the East and you look towards the West you will see every thing in full light and totally without shadow, because you see them from the same side as the sun: and if you look towards the South or the North you will see all objects in light and shade, because you see both the side towards the sun and the side away from it; and if you look towards the coming of the sun all objects will show you their shaded side, because on that side the sun cannot fall upon them."

If you type that sentence out, you will see that the author was thinking about looking at things at different times and he liked thinking about that so much he didn't want his sentence to stop, so he held it together in Italian and it still holds together in English and it is an informative and beautiful sentence especially to someone who has a hard time knowing where she is and is amazed by someone knowing where things are including the cardinal directions.

~

J is painting the birch stump green by pressing grass and violets' leaves into the wood and rubbing them in. Dandelion and mustard greens are also part of the paint. In the morning he took apart, then restored, the pile of wood around the maple tree. Now he made purple on the page by rubbing violets' petals on it. "I'm in the mood for an experiment with nature's colors." Hen pokes her head in front of mine to see: are these words something she can eat. In the sun, her comb is scarlet red.

~

A dress for the carnival.

What da Vinci says is "To make a beautiful dress cut it in cloth and give it an odoriferous varnish, made of oil of turpentine and varnish in grain, with a pierced stencil, which must be wetted, that it may not stick to the cloth; and this stencil may be made in a pattern of knots which afterward may be filled up with black, and the ground with white millet."

He says (writes) it in Italian. A pretend dress. But the decorative element and pattern (black & white millet grains glued onto cloth) would be even more material than what they're creating the illusion of: "knots" "embroidered" on cloth.

There are three instructions for setting fires, such as how to set a room on fire safely: "Suddenly you will see the room in a blaze like a flash of lightning, and it will do no harm to anyone." First you take away "that yellow surface which covers oranges and distill them in an alembic, until the distillation may be said to be perfect." Then the orange will be on fire, like the rooms he describes before and after in separate paragraphs. Envision the orange, he might be thinking, as a cosmos, room or stanza, depending on where you are in the translation.

~

With one person I've experienced a whispering gallery to work, the night my snake bracelet disappeared. Accuracy was a pleasure, knowing your way around the city as I would if the city were made of grammar.

My feeling is that I shot Jack when he went senile and yowled all night unfortunately just after the baby started sleeping after three years of no sleep for anyone. It was not possible for me to continue to not sleep; it was time to kill the cat but I didn't kill him. I held him while the vet injected him and wept the whole time his body froze and hardened under my hands. We had Jack 15 years and he was 19 when he died. So a cat and a horse and a dog are buried here, plus 34 chickens and all the animals killed by the dog, raccoons, and other predators. The horse is the funniest story of all, how he died and got buried (he wasn't ours), but I tell it only in social settings when there is nothing else to tell.

Do you like winter anymore. Where one is trellised in a manuscript, a letter <u>A</u>, black socks I'm sorry to have borrowed so long. Oh song she some time said. The trees have rings in them. The lines around the yew go around as if the whole time we were there.

"Experience shows us that the air must have darkness beyond it and yet it appears blue."

A doctor is working to stabilize my pelvis. Excellent. Largely this appears to be about breath, inhaling as you extend the limbs, exhaling to contract. Because the body is 3-dimensional: breath going in and down not just the "front" of you but also down the spine into the low back, sacrum, and so on. The question of whether there is always something erotic going on.

"If you want to make foreshortened letters stretch the paper in a drawing frame and then draw your letters and cut them out, and make the sunbeams pass through the holes on to another stretched paper, and then fill up the angles that are wanting."

~

The rest of the morning.
tomorrow
today
tonight

"a bird with wings akimbo appears to be sliding down a stretched string. On a diagonal."

The wind and the rain.

~

Transcribed to be read aloud

Of the muscles of animals
Of the lions, when bent.
Of trees and lights on them
Of the houses of a town
Of representing wind
The wind
Of the scars on trees.
Of the ramification.
Of the accidents of colouring in trees.
Of the visibility of these accidents.
Of the 4 points of the Compass.
Of the spaces (showing the sky) in trees themselves.
Of trees which conceal these spaces in one another.

Of the "motion of the surface of the water which resembles that of hair, and has two motions, of which one goes on with the flow of the surface, the other forms the lines of eddies; thus the water forms eddying whirlpools one part of which are due to the impetus of the principal current and the other to the incidental motion and return flow."

Inching toward sleep—now go.

I don't think we've answered the question, what's all that desire <u>for</u>.

~

Compost—decay

"On a walk I see . . .
"I was walking along the river and . . . [this happened]

And look: look outside . . .

aware of themselves—
    body/machine

colons . . .
does punctuation become the joints

~

they all add up to instructions
on your eyelids
no more love poems
this isn't a love poem
these words
in the world!

~

Rain at 4 a.m.
Some letters dream them

People around a door, saying their names.
The names ended with <u>man</u> or <u>men</u>.
The night before that, people who died, talking to each other.

~

The sun appears to have gotten closer to the window because the light through it
intensified.

I'd like to see a peregrine falcon, knowing it really was a peregrine falcon.

Birds I mistake for other birds
would be a long list
repeating itself.

I doubt I will ever become a crane.

~

Many people have heard a cat speak once, and perhaps other animals as well.
This proves animals can use words, they just choose not to do so—for their
whole lives in most cases. They're like monks who've taken a vow of silence with
such dedication we imagine they don't speak.

Every day the little horse
rides past me on its bike, the little horse thinks
as it runs across the pasture to the fence along the road, then runs away.

~

Clouds over Lake Michigan can hide all Fools and knaves because their hair is
like Queen Margaret's cow. Ahoy! No more fingers in my ears! A mother dreams
of dolphins making noise with their big-eyed bodies.

~

Found

"On a map, this tiny route in Cincinnati looks like someone began to make a
cross street connecting two avenues then decided better of it and gave up. It's
actually a staircase going up a hill."

~

James just observed, "That diary is sad, isn't it?" *Mourning Diary*. Yes. "Maybe
I'll write one when you die." Laughter. "I will!" Laughter. "I'll start it early! A
fictional one! 'Yesterday, Maman died.'"

~

Dandelion says
thinking of mushrooms? in the sun
because we just uncovered them

+

the face of the sun's imprinted on the wood
even though it was covered all winter

6 years ago we pressed a bunch of dandelion stems
into the bark and rubbed them in
to "paint" the stump green, and it's still green
& the flat sawn top is purple
from crushed-up violets rubbed in too

The stump's behind the white pine
between the dawn redwood Henry planted
& the witch hazel Andy planted
which makes me think of Amy Jo
Trier-Walker, her lucky name
for a tree farmer and a walker

J sold all his beans
at market today, $42
for Tiger's Eye, Black Turtle & Hutterite Soup
Right now it's too windy
for seedlings in their tray—
green pepper seedlings, each the width
of twelve hair's-breadths, top-heavy
w/tapered oval-triangle leaves
The seeds were put with tweezers
in connecting square-inch boxes
like ice trays full of soil, soon to be moved outside

We were in the desert, now I'm in the orchard

In the desert was a cactus ringed with colors
having spun around it really fast
as it fell from outer space

in the middle of a conversation

~

da Vinci again

Drawings of furnaces
many designs for knots,
a head of Christ done with pen,
Several compositions of Angels,
[. . .]
Some pitchers seen in perspective
Some machines for ships,
Several throats of old women,
Several heads of old men,
Several nude figures, complete,
Head of Our Lady ascending into Heaven,
    A head with a hat on,
    A representation of the Passion, a cat,
    A head of a girl with her hair gathered in a knot.

~

day before yesterday

bright snow in the woods?
giant nest of twigs, three feet in diameter, made by a person sitting in the snow?

lines of the trail map on the wooden rectangle of the post outside the woods?

Wind-tunnel grief is a howl
Get up and cook something

~

first night at the beekeeper's
raw goat-milk yogurt
raw fermented honey soda

melons were
in the FIELD
planted by Henry and Lotte
go back and try again

~

Transcribed from the Speech Accent Archive

Please call Stella. Ask her to bring
these things with her from the store:
Six spoons of fresh snow peas, five
thick slabs of blue cheese, and maybe

a snack for her brother Bob. We also
need a small plastic snake and a big
toy frog for the kids. She can scoop
these things into three red bags, and we will go
meet her Wednesday at the train station.

~

& drew that eye-shape with you in it
being the place of my solitude

whether the summer bugs around the light are
insects or wizards, I fold the house up like a crease
and go outside

something blue-green like the number 5
pent self, impresencing
your and my

~

The palm of the hand is as square as a house
to set a triangle on top of.
Plus two smaller squares inside
for windows. A rectangle door.
I do not say this to the tree
waving all of its arms.
The tree says nothing
that I built
that I remember

drawing such houses
who have no hands
speak clearly

~

The shadow had a use
for the possum, the ruffed grouse and the rabbit

Her head was full of crumbs and gears

Never stand on a ladder
standing on icy snow
now Henry's knees
are full of bees

"I think that the Root of the Wind is Water"

& now I see you washed your hair
in Dorothy Wordsworth's journals
"washed your head"
is what they said

~

farm objects are
around me so I put them here
& breathing fool
the implements

vaginal rocks & animal sky
I noticed outside Los Angeles

did anyone
feed the kittens and their snaggle-toothed mother
who showed up a week before they were born
all five and their seven names

the skate park's a concrete oasis
in the shape of waves, all to ourselves in the morning
plus the mower, mowing around

across the hall from
being about to
look for a brain fire not about love

envelopes used to be small
in the interest of making a whirl'd

stone at your back's a midpoint for the wind comes through
two accounts of this twinship, little cabbage in the shoe

~

"While You Were Out"

Pennywhistle
Gulls
Traffic wash-up

Car horns here and there
Another car needing a muffler
Harley engine good sound

Spring buds on
flowering trees

Out loud in class Christell I think
said Please forgive me
if I can't read my handwriting

     *

We're still in
the garden
with the motors
and the engines
YES I can hear
the rake against
the dirt and
grass.

The sun feels good
right here. There was more about a
leaf-blower but the
pages
blew away.

    ~

Seventh grade assignment sheet comes out from under
the driver's seat, crumpled & muddy on the backseat floor

    "Choose at least six of the following:
    Construct a golden rectangle, chaos ball, etc."

~~and the motion was like breathing~~

   ~

Notes

1. Child running. (Woman running?)
person running
out of the frame,
caught moment of
movement on a plane of
snow. Light on the snow
too, so the picture
is a picture of stillness
and speed. Stone? Step.
Stone steps in the background.
I just bought pants for
a friend and my umbrella
kept opening in the street.
West 15th.

2. The notebook I wanted
was for music

MUSIC, it said on the front
with a large grace note for
illustration. I wanted it for
writing in but it cost $6.95.
James says he sleeps in a cello bed
& he can hear it singing in his sleep, he says.

3. ~~I like these pictures of~~
Snow. (Snow?) The whales are
swimming farther north because
of melting. The flood
prevention systems in place
in London "were not designed
to deal with climate change."
In Southern Utah the rock—
desert of rock—
had been fully under water.

4. Wing half out of the frame—one
of 2 wings, of a butterfly
or hang-glider or fancy kite.

5. A window elsewhere
A curved ~~(arch~~
and inset window (arch)
divided into five square panes
and a half-moon on top
to fit the arch. You called
just now so you become

part of the picture.
I'm seeing him in his
borrowed funeral clothes
and a picture of the window
and adjusting
the ice pack on my back.
Jane and Heiko
or Jonny and Sarah
might have taken this picture.

6. Write to me.

7. Real mountains. Or ink
lithographs. Old print
or postcard detail
or c.g.i.
Yet you will grieve
and know why.
When my father sent
his first wife's ashes to her
parents in Japan
the ashes were returned with a note
saying she was
already dead & was dead
since she married him
the dirty jew
photographer, my father.

8. The top stroke of a
Chinese ideogram, maybe

part of a word such as the word
energy or element or
entity or
thing hanging in place.
Arms outstretched,
person in red, nice
hands in gloves.
An arm's length a fathom
both arms outstretched
full fathom? Fly.

9. The End. The glacial
tunnel
Wernerian doctrine (Thales?)
that all life began in water
as water

~

The child drew lines in a rounding curve and said: This is a pigeon asking a
question. He drew a blot under it and said: This is a question mark.

~~As~~
~~The~~ man ~~cut peppers   poured oil on~~
~~the peppers simmered in the~~
The man poured oil on the peppers.

The woman walked backward
toward the lake.

(Does it have to be true?)

About your way in reading a poem of being alive . . .

~

And: the rhyme is a hand Bell-made, bell-wrung, un-Chaste in coming back as if to Dig the Edges of the word's own Flickeringly comprehended Grave. Agamben, did you say? Hop up, my Ladies into the June, or In Jest the 14 Knives did glimmer Like a spring in Spring. My word, the Night is an Octagon, an Opiate, an Other Page in Quiet if we open to the Ruse. It's hard to Say, to say that is a sen-Tence or Umbrellical cord in-Viting Without motive. So does a Xylophone undo the sense and Yoke it like a letter, Zim to zam to zoom.

From the apartment James carries apples and grapes to Sylvie down the street. She likes Ruby Jon, the purple apple with a star inside when you cut it as J instructed me to do when he came home from school. Should kids go to school when they are five. I was surprised to see the pattern inside even though I knew a star pattern was inside. We cut the apple into cup-shaped halves, good to eat except for the prickly star part.

~

An internal window divides the front porch from a room. The room has a 60-dollar piano from beside the railroad tracks, a crate of records, a record player with one speaker, and a bamboo chair from Goodwill in Janesville. Because of the old piano & the record player, the room is called the music room.

In summer the internal window stays open and it's possible to climb from the chair in the music room through the window onto the porch.

Around the corner and behind the door is a hollow-body guitar Leif gave James for safe-keeping or for keeps, however it turns out. In thanks, J wrote "Dear Leaf, my mother saw a downy woodpecker." Before the guitar was moved behind the door, it vibrated audibly in its case when anyone walked past it.

~

Storm light: singular
yellow sky

Enter with bell

Practice the kiss with Robert, jumping up
after sitting down

Pin wigs, fix ladder, find shoe

~

Others could tell the difference
btwn the tones of bees from different hives
Carniolan & Italian, but I couldn't

Each of us held a queen
in a box and lowered her down
to the top-bar hives Andy made

Four boxes of bees into four hives
= 4 queens
12,000 bees in all

I hadn't planned to help, felt dropped
in the orchard by accident, because of the bees'
vibrational hum

~

night day night

a tiny museum fits in the cap
a mushroom pushes up
the basement stairs

wanting to read and eat the plants
but didn't come near

oh sorry about
the onion breath
the moon's getting
to be half-full

~

Instructed to move the bees who'd swarmed, we could see about 4,000 clustered
to a branch. Henry planned to cut the branch, drop it quickly into a bucket,
cover the bucket and move the swarm to a new hive we'd already made from a
barrel. But the bees were gone when we got to the tree.

Now I can collect the honey, unless the bees have merely <u>split</u> the hive—in which case half would return and need their honey for winter.

The feeling that living with bees promotes the production of sweet sticky fluids unspun from inside the body and thru it, and that this bears comparison with Blake's description in *Visions of the Daughters of Albion*.

~

In the morning
you see what you say:
    Don't get breastmilk on the newspaper

Having moved out so she could read a book
having imagined moving out so she could read a book

the mother rolled a ball across the floor
the ball was a bell again

~

I could remember a small amount
but the forest was full of felled trees
and tangled clothing about the leaves

It's necessary to learn the prepositions first
J discovers, because of where things are

I don't trust any form of birth control
but end rhymes are a pleasure

for example H is building a tower
of blocks to be knocked down

Astrologically the garden's a disaster
but we can correct this with an Ephemeris

as if the internal crowds out the external
as in the Revolution according to Turgenev

the arms go around
the various shades

~

airplane womb sound
no one's floating.
only the mind

what's between halves of the rib cage
everything
stinking

~

All winter couldn't fit outside a book
I wrote in 2011

Come now permission to gather
in five kinds, meticulous

for seedpods, keeping & sorting
with tweezers in the dirt

kid gets covered by dirt w/probably some cat pee in the mix

~

Abbott Road
Rose Street
Grand Avenue
Gunson Street
Grand & Dale
[L. A. street]
Emigration Canyon Road
East 81st
Central Ave.
State Road 213

~

where are the bees

Queen Claritas &
Queen Calamitous
crash into the end of the notebook
sticky with pinesap and cedar leaves

the book is a Sound-House somewhere

~

Catalogues are full of pictures
seeds & plants
past the fraying, in the present
snowfall of the winter of our first return
we covered the berries with straw
and the number of places we've lived
"your beauty, which I lost sight of once . . ." (Levertov)

Two dreams in one

Didn't bring enough food for lunch.
Was everybody there.
I saw that
shape you
made with your ear.
It was inside.

~

Beginning with a silver pencil, part of the curtain folds over itself.

Blue nailpolish on Sam's toes and blue honey from the candy factory she told about.

We heard <u>ocean</u> and <u>propane</u> in the flowerpot and suddenly we gathered our things and ran away.

The succulent has a C-curve in its spine and Shiva arms. It bends away from the light and reaches out in lots of ways.

~

On the Beara Peninsula
with my love the trees
are the alphabet many things
this notebook of graph paper
came from there—half a euro
who is in it—you are sort of
before it's gone

~

Completion an instant
if you finish

The palm forest burned around
ATLANTIC
OCEAN
the child drew

~

Spotted Winged Drosophila. New pest with bad fairy name, which does this: makes a pin-prick hole in the new blue skin of blueberries just at the moment the berry ripens. Inserts its larva in the center of the berry and the larva grows and the fruit turns to mush from the inside out. Nothing helps except picking green or poisoning the whole bush. Canada's wild blueberries & Maine's & other northern places' may not have SWD because of colder winters. For a while.

~

I would like some sea salt if you have some sea salt.

The star fish, first called <u>sea star</u>—its five points being "arms"—the starfish being armless

Why stars are drawn having "points" when they are pointless—call Stella, etcetera

Would you like a painting to be on
a word, a body to be in
a lithe word
ridden on its rims
"sticks thrust in its spokes"
all together rid of
foliage
the toad most resembled a stone
for camouflage concealed it like a stone
a theory of rhyme being offered

~

James is pounding copper
making a ring for the ocean
slipped it off

~

Have sent a point from out
so far   the tide re-
turned to deepen in
and slipping
on the slick steps down
to water I
salt scattered fell

~

Who will confess that
in a bad time

some riven and
arriving
stone sound's clear
for the waves
go back to beginning
with a

breaking
over the rocks

~

Misheard <u>what</u> and <u>why</u>
for <u>wheat</u> and <u>rye</u>

Under the ground is an actual river
J "cuts the grass" with scissors

~

There were insects in the amber
bracelet of my mother
house after house

~

May ever any thing come in
around the heart under the bones that
touch each other in the town and in the
yellow-breasted woodpecker or a golden
sky gets big outside the eye, if you have any
Appaloosa horses in your self   do try
to plant some hops beside the barn and carry
fescue in your arms

~

Mid-May to September

(Cultivated fields,
fencerows, shores,
thickets, waste places)

Bunch
Clump
Cluster
Bale
Bundle

~

A note from my mother in the '70s

    Hi, Honey
    I borrowed $8 from your Snoopy bank
    and will be at the Ashram until
    9 or so.

    ~

The night is <u>rustling</u> outside the window.

III.

Summer, 2015

yes eros being eros but for what
is it for this
vibration being trumpet under streamers as the hills go
toward the matter but an onion
flowers wild in the two worlds on an axis
which is only what it looks like—life form
the lecherous
asparagus
towers over the sun

    *

a notebook divides
between bodies, observing
water is animal:
when you enter the water, you enter its body
of course it's alive
& all the things in it aren't separate
the names don't matter
what's being
alive

    *

scattered up from the ground the lightning
seemed to fishtail in Ohio
through the hot green grass outside a Shell
Mobil
or something

*

July 1

Flying warrior in the raspberries
in order to pick the raspberries
because of asparagus five feet high

Something gets written
because it's begun

*

Changing a little
what J. K. wrote
& leaving stuff out

Who wants to hear about milkweed?
If neighbors complain, show them the bees
just move over, rolling or falling
from one to the next

Marvelous gentle the bees

*

a person walks by and is cooling
the air however slightly in the walking
it sometimes tips me over

fall down and write

stop trying
to make an idea
where the face comes in
to focus
to flow past
some other thing dream love this
time being with you

     *

yes we'll clean the theater, patch & plaster

what do you dream about
now that it's over: the play
& everyone in it

     *

o clever o flying o monkey o may some

time be

golden in the measure of a

breath   hand   spiny tail

of the horseshoe crab

*

the sun is on my face
pressing these the words in

no thank you for the eye pillow

change the first Sutra   now
is a redundant word

feet legs ankles
someone walks by

I am a half frog & stick out my tongue

*

August 12

Is laughter any words that are not words
inside the tree, a lot of noise
like when you put your ear
on someone's stomach—abdomen
all that going on
coursing through
longing the body
of each tree   lengthening

but I was tumbling
around the ocean, in the ocean
full of one

vibration after another
felt on my eyelids
the sun saying who
walked to shore without a word
found a stone
that isn't beautiful
it's for the sill

    *

After the beach

a part of the book opened under the other part, like those books with holes cut
into them so that instead of pages there are jewels

James is reading
<u>J</u> is a good sound but not the reason for his name
<u>L</u> is a little *la di da*   <u>F</u> disappears

we don't know what tree we're sitting under—light green lichen on gray bark
he asks me not to fart
that word makes this a Zen poem
it often appears

    *

August 13

Marsh grass is fluorescent green
just after the tide goes out
Marsh grass is called eel grass, but I didn't
swim across the channel

just lay in the mud & waited
Sun comes back
when the sunflower turns
not that there are sunflowers
here among the tidal pools
something wishes to be true
Mushrooms were bright yellow
and the blueberries were blue

Discover Didot typeface
has more space between each letter

I had no Kabbalah poems for the editor
How many melons did Henry sell, we'll find out later

Fill the green glass boat with water

    *

August 14

Why say "telling time"
Who's for singing
into the dolphin
Those are the shoulders being put right
in their sockets as you taught us
There's a pen that can write upside down
pineapple cake
it can write in outer space

I'm writing on the bus of course
from Boston to New York
did five Seagull Breaths in the station
and Half-Moon sort of
Sunday morning
all the news

Even so, stretching outside Burger King
The bus takes a break
No one leaves the bus for the sun
It's 103   I like it, the parkinglot-sized hotflash

There goes the woman who peed on the seat
Everything noticed is greeting
I pray to the little god eros

        *

August 16

Another insect to talk to
goes on the pinecone under the spruce.
I'm on a plane that can't move
because LaGuardia lost power.
If I remember what the insect was—half
remembered, imagined, may the day
itself come back

Wake up slowly from the lift-off doze
big blurry trance

La La wonder man
don't sit down on the Turnpike
nobody said

    *

August 29

Transformation makes nothing happen
16-foot golden body of the cricket or whoever
you think you're hearing now.

I miss the play
full of words that were not mine, but I became
Miss La Creevey, Julia Wititterly, Captain Adams
Dr. Lumbey, Second Milliner, Young Woman, Seventh Boy, and the Keeper
of the Madman who threw vegetables
over the wall.

    *

August 31

Were you to meet her ever again.

Not jagged, ear down
to the ground and out, a slow
face likely, from you yourself or the other way around.

A crow's upset between the house and river.

About the clanging just now added to the crow
something being dug or smashed, getting louder, getting done.

"It starts behind the heart, extending thru fingertips on both hands."

She came and lay down
while I was sleeping
right here in this bed
& pressed her memory, some memories, into mine,
the dead author whose letters I read.

Do you think this can happen
a good sleep making space for others

    *

Wish for more than one name.

Writing w/a yellow marker, to be ever so slightly
Sydney Carton, although I am not.

Tune comes in.
Old tune in the beautiful mouth.
Cubs fans are happy on the train that can't move.
I'll close my eyes and stop writing, on the not-moving train & the moving train
What's the disease, graphomania? How are the animals

    *

Finding the lion inside the book, a lion
heart shifts

line waits to appear
    NO BREATH AFTER FIVE, the choirmaster
tells the boys

    *

the necklace—most common meal—one time—what he loved—

her name and her name an other name, an other's name is her other name.
A lion-colored day has no name
under grass, earth and within
the fire-throated core

not saying time

cooling now in the tenth month
with the eighth name
before winter
ever

    *

Heart is in the vertebrae
and you read it sideways

Part of a pig had cooked in
the pot from which we drank
sugar-water w/violets & dandelions
boiled to serve the bees

James's ear is an Irish stone
then draw the heart no bones

Out the window is it
sunny in Detroit

Heart is in the fingertips
almost always quietly

    *

Sun come down
Poisonous rays and all

Stick your whole face in a melon
You have broken apart w/your hands

That is the reason
A moth's blue or yellow in the world

                  messenger
                  melons were

"in the hollow of your throat"

go back and try again

    *

Rain on the rooftop cousin
woke me up at 3 a.m.
The arms legs torso of the child
are full of bites and sweaty
so scooch away from the vise grip
but his breath is cooling

    *

Carrie said what a fig is:
a flower turned inside out

Once a melon landed on the head
of an old man on a bus
It fell from the luggage rack
Lucky he laughed

and the cliffs dropt down to the sea

    *

weird fire way to breathe

accordion mind for the folding-
into-each-other-sounds and
their stretching out again harmonics
becomes this
feeling of reading I have it rarely

    *

7 poplars by the water
unrelated to 7 in other poem
Eros is loud here don't run away

IV.

"Preserving a Sand Mandala"

(Denver Art Museum)

"How do you preserve a mandala made entirely of loose sand? How do you move it into an elevator and take it up five stories in the museum without destroying the design? The answer is 'consolidation.' Museum conservators consolidated—or glued together—the loose grains of sand by applying adhesive in the fine mist. They used a slow-drying solvent that allowed the adhesive to settle between the grains of sand before it hardened. This prevented a shiny crust from forming on the surface and ensured that the mandala's appearance would not be altered by the consolidation process.

"Museum curators applied about 50 coats of adhesive during a two-week period. A plastic tent slowed the drying process and constrained the adhesive mist, which is toxic. Conservators also wore gloves and facemasks to protect themselves.

"After treatment, museum staff could lift and move the sand mandala without damaging it."

The mandala was made in 1996 by monks of the Seraje Monastery.

~

Orfordville, 2006

The task of naming the dragonfly weighed heavily on the child, who'd just discovered the concepts <u>police</u>, <u>jail</u>, <u>law</u>. The latter two were mysterious but the first he understood. "Police will get you," he'd say on the heels of expressing a forbidden desire (to ride without a car seat, to walk too far into the waves, to play in the parking garage by himself), all because she once told him the police would stop them if he didn't ride in his car seat. She said that although they would get a ticket, they would not be taken to jail. Years later, they talked about race, or skin color, and why, for example, her half-brother, his uncle, had a taser pointed at him by police while he was walking our mother's dog. Earlier though, when asked to explain <u>jail</u>, she said it is a small room from which one is not permitted to leave. "Remember police?" he began to say to her and others; "police will take you to jail." From then on, the concepts burst from him with increasing frequency in what she called the instinct of precaution, evasion and escape all at once.

*

The dragonfly kept appearing at the start of things, as I am hungry for a large lunch of lambsquarters, radish, and whatever else appears on the ground. Our hike is composed of illusion, I said to the child when he demanded first the sea, then the river he thought promised by the horizon, which opened rather on "cash crops" and the silvery not-sea (road). We/I offered the child birch bark and shale shards + handfuls of berries along the trail.

~

Time does oscillate Aha
so summer apologizes down inside

nighttime eerie love yes
everytime hippocrates sings.
motherlike terrace downward edge

RAGGED PEACE NOW
JESTS RIGHT BY
LUCK INSIDE SOME
CLOUD

the animals will speak seven languages for two weeks.

If you couldn't remember what winter was,

the difference between laughter and something invisible

~

landscape

observation of

insouciance

it was nervous

Or, it was your deepest brightest secret.

Is it true that all our failures can be said to be failures of love

~

Each letter begins with the alphabet. It forgets.

Beguile me, I was thinking, when thinking what could Stevens have been think-ing when he heard "be thou me" or "bethou me"—what have I bethought me, that to thy purpose bows?

This is not about that.

~

Extract what you were looking at in every love letter you ever wrote, I mean the soy fields, guy sleeping on bus, boy riding cow, nothing but air, red blossom, yel-low shirt, of course the light through maple leaves, many leaves, person crossing street, praying mantis doing T'ai Chi, or were you hearing all those things

One vowel turns to another, turns into another and that's a lot going on all the time.

~

The rest of the notebook appears to be notes on the Two-Part *Prelude* of 1799

   3 Qs: to lines 26. Magical form?
   Begins as questions.
   water/voice—dreams—maternal origin—substitute?
   thoughts & knowledge (mind)—nature, earth

Music
composition
   3rd Q: earth, air, water, fire—all elements.
   self in nature.
   What has happened? to line 49
   feeling
[. . .]
Book 5—Books—dream—Geometry & Shell
   Boy of Winander l. 389

Brooke

   ~

When the wild onion floats on its back in the half-day light

and the yellow hen stops arguing with her god

in the winter, early winter, just past light.

Pencil presses halfway
and the time of time is short

   ~

Many lines around the eyes
had been the sun having its way

   CROWS! Out of the vines

~

Observation of pattern, detail of
life forms—plants, trees, insects, animals
human
letters
      whirl'd form / world from
akin to

What is Pastoral? not up to it.

Not of the self.
"Memory has no place."
Investigation.
No I.
Nor Virgil.
"Making with material reality
in extraordinary particularity."

Rukeyser, *Book of the Dead*
Browne, *Garden of Cyrus*
Césaire, "Poetry and Knowledge"
Lucida / Berkeley poems / what's the action
see the making
of the pré

Helsinki Window—Creeley in Finland
In what world
is everyone here

~

Transcriptions from unknown sources

"There is a kind of story, God, that glides along under everything else that is happening, and this kind of story only jumps out into the light like a silver fish when it wants to see where it lives in relation to everything else." 12–13

"Everything that has form is also a mathematical secret and has to move very quickly to avoid being solved." 223

~

In Avoca, I said <u>field</u>
but heard it's <u>prairie</u>

Watching it walking
(both bodies moving)
saw it unfold,
unfield

~

remember 2 days
from now?

It does, the sound,
seem to get
bigger, and to

combine with
airplanes and car horns.
Trees. Train.
throat-singing person-friend crabapple tree

THROAT-SINGING PERSON-FRIEND CRABAPPLE TREE

~

Here a pen draws a line through, and squiggly lines go over, what had just begun to be written. The order of sentences is easily mixed up. Elizabeth Barrett in the margin of her Bible: "I have hurried thru' my life like a shuttle." Too many to feel it's honest to pinpoint one. Too much of a jumble.

~

Salzburg translations

Until over-going's objective, first:
and some can ski for a minute.
That ends with a sacred some-way intermittent.
Willingly glad I ate second of it.
That monster I fire? Loft,
sang not lofty, in loft-madness,
simple sang. Hand by hand the
salt-king's boat, hand-piece laid home.
Jagged will scoot farther-not-any one island.
That are so.
Make it some hand before the small oar then.

Fasten, like-veil, and mold it in minute—
Slam I made my fine-grade sign.
I melt it in four, and ring.
No, I will into gift-me, medium
dig. Yes Yes.
Jagged stars have stammered,
that minute-tuned. Yeah,
I alter my net.

~

I mean any position of the mouth is
open if you let it
as when Nathan, Peter Joe and Henry
went to Dolci's Donuts
and Peter Joe had a cicada
in his mouth, so when he opened it to speak
the cicada flew right out

and when the sun is bending on its knee
perhaps to ask what we propose
without the planet as we know it,
catastrophe complete,
selva fastened to its absence, forest to a shadow
Ghost forest, ocean, planet, ghost

"therefore all seasons shall be sweet to thee"

thee are an other

if animals press into you at night—let Josie the dog sleep in the bed

Josie's eyes are like my dad's, I've thought

Josie looks like Lisa, Fin said

then they picked apples

then they sorted apples

~

Parody of 18thc Rationalism lines 805   ⟶

knife—body—truth   lines 870   ⟶   p. 406

he re-tells it around 660 (p. 394)

so doing he subverts the fiction of

historical progress(ion)

Last letter? or 1 more due next wk . . .

The Weather at 6:00 . . .

~

Inside, read what you wrote.

Now take each piece of paper

off the pink pad ("While You Were Out")

& shuffle randomly. Read/hear.

Spread them all out. Make a new arrangement.

Read/hear.

Some of you have 2 absences.
Several of you have 1.

~

The number 1 under the belly of the deer, drawn in pencil by a child.

The frames (frame?) of somebody's glasses.

Monday I saw a dead bee inside a grape I was about to pick from the vine.

Also: instructions

~~I suppose this is how she managed not to~~

~

On the Beara Peninsula

The shadow of the mountain moved across the mountain quickly, very quickly because the wind was blowing the cloudmass fast, so it looked as if another mountain were forming and disappearing or as if the mountain itself were moving as Dōgen thought: Mountains walk, he said, not referring to geologic processes by which mountains change; both green and white mountains walk. In this case the mountain was running, not walking—its name is Maulin and we may climb it on J's birthday, before it runs away.

*

Approaching Maulin in thick fog all day, we expected it to be another peak, then found it no higher than our knees. Between Maulin and another ridge bordering Eyeries I was brought to the waterfall, which does not look anything like what it is from any kind of distance, even a short distance.

*

Five trees in the Ogham alphabet were everywhere in the forest today, three for sure and I only don't know if I can identify an alder or a hazel.

*

It's 11 p.m. and still not dark, here in Lauragh by the river with the alder rowan holly birch or hazel on June 7. At the stone circle J left a piece of quartz resembling the jawbone of an ass, he said, surrounded by sheep and the dead. He played a D scale on the *feadog* or tin whistle, possibly Irish flute.

*

Sit on a stone in the sun
in the grass and flame-yellow gorse
in the wind and the moon comes up.

*

A fair swimming letter, an unidentified tree.

Only six to eight of the 20 letters in the Ogham alphabet are tree names, despite Robert Graves's excitement about an entire tree alphabet in which every word, all writing, would consist of various combinations of trees.

One letter that's not a tree can be translated as "fair swimming letter." The letter is pronounced the same as the Gaelic word for salmon (*èbad*), just as our letter o is pronounced the same as the word oh.

Since then I've been reminded that there's no stillness in matter at all at the molecular level. It seems likely that the extent to which apparently stationary things are moving we may not see, or know we're seeing. Could we do so, the distinction between "plant" and "animal" as different life forms might emerge, along with many other things, as a simple but enormous mistake.

V.

"your shoulder"
& bike grease on the white blouse, derailleur-pressed
her back like that
all the clothes getting caught in
machines & plants--grew in the field
a shirt of flax
Grew in the forest, pine bread & sap
press together
~~write: our mouth.~~

So a glance can fall on <u>duration</u>, mind flit to <u>adoration</u>
See with your hands not just your eyes I said to James in the berries
same as woodwork or clay
He added: piano, guitar   pauses at
The eye~~xsweepxsxup~~   swee ps the room, the litter
~~litter~~ of maps from the drawers of the oak being emptied   later
of countries, counties, cit ies, orchards, listed also
alphabetically (Star Orchard, Star Valley Orchards, Starry Ridge
Orchard, Strojny Orchard . . .Therns Apples, Theys Orchard,
Tom-Dooley Orchard, Viney Farms, Whispering Orchard, Zickert Orchard)
~~& litter of~~ cl ips, keys, butts, VCR manual, w arranties,
Rubber bands
Must ~~write~~ furiously, hearing you open the door
      type

to the house below, no one awake until now

The deer llay under
the wheel a n instant

James "cut the grass" with scissors
on top of an underground river
Seven miles west of here, pearls filled the Sugar River
Strangley were insects inside the beads
Barbara my mother's amber bracelet
freckled wrist
necklace
East of Edgerton South of Madison
Union two is unincorporated

Where is the shirt taken off by the way
side of the house
thief who broke in
the night before my levitation
in the light up the streetfrom an open
magnolia tree

of

sp
ad

te
xt

road from   down

next pg.

East of Edgerton South of Madison
Union

A little further up the road
Union is unincorporated
is
Union further up the road is too unincorporated
is too unincorporated
East of Edgerton South of Madison
The fox too lays under

What the bird's nest was made of:
          straw (primarily)
          baling wire--1 thin silver/gray wire
          oragge twine (ours) from the orchard or barn)
          long black hair from a horse's tail (about 2 of these)
          1 strip of ribbon used for gift-wrapping--light blue
               and white checked, about 1 centimeter in width.
               This ribbon was unruly in the nest, popping out
               of it and curling out, unfurling, giving a look
               of whimsy and decoration to the bowl of mostly straw.

Sizeof next: not large, slightly smaller than two hands cupped
          together (my hands).

Where found: center of back yard on the ground. Could have fallen
          from the White Pine (5eneedles per needle pod) or the
          hickory, from which xxxgxxthe used to hang the sky chair.

     What kind of bird: ???

Now when I brush my hair I take the hair out of the brush and
instead of putting in the compost container on the xkixsink,
I put it oùtside in the grass for bxi birds to find and use.
Would like to find a nest and maybe catch sight of myme strands
of mine in its construction. If I have some of another person's
hair then both of ours could end up being part of one

March 25, 2012

The drumming bird's harder to hear than songbirds, & harder to see
(A flicker drums into the cambium layer)
Child plays strings in the grass band

Entire form of a day
or kestrel once perched on a branch -- not naming trees
I follow a line
from a door to a door
drawing a music it trembles

You can put the pollen in your mouth and eat it, biting it out of the blossom
usually in May, this year in March

What stops the writing is violence
--why Brenda wrote "violins"? kept in the meaning of measure?

Laura went (Riding) in Jackson-
ville Florida
ill Florida
She was not shot
walking or driving

You can suck the juice out of frozen apples on the branch all winter
Bees keep to the cambium layer
in larger trees outside the orchard

Don't think of them as trees
Her body fit entirely inside his body
Pine bark in pine bread's eaten in Sweden

We cut and smoothed a number of apple boughs
on which to hange"filtering" curtains
A branch makes an uneven line,ppart tree this side of the window

She put glasses on the scarecrow
four inches high made of clover

Who are the letters
in the doorway or do I
start drawing
lines in the facing page
lens face appearing place
the wishing swept into a boat
When you see the rhyme the water floats

Laughter thought her
out

 Winter over
Clothes put by
in the cedar trunk
First phallus popped up: asparagus
in the land of the rabbits

Unlike an owl
~~need you near~~
~~to see with~~

move

Beans

Bush

Black valentine ✓

Hutterite soup ✓

~~Cylypso~~ :(didn't hoe enough

Painted pony ✓

Brown dutch ✓ :)

Peregion ✓

~~Adzuki~~ :)

lowa's champion lost 1/2 rotted

tigers eye ✓ very pretty / needs more hoeing

Pole

cherookee trail of tears

Hadatsa sheild figure

Turkeys Craw

Jmney

beans, beans
the ...

Black Coco?
Large oval

some missing from list!

+ Black Turtle?
Small

In the a possible dark we were reading
nothing of words
they are handling
there is no f easier to see
What is the name without the face
feeling handled
wanting to
past the face
and not having out from under
any of a reach's own face
possible

Saxifrage, wonders Anglo—
What is that—dear students
it is a plant I think
part musical
instrument part flower

what is what

the lover is one who reads
nothing but words
and hands them
past the face

the lover is one who reads
art of words
and hands them
past the face

words balance you (?)
then you see

VI.

At the same time as scattering

The train goes through this borough on the island is it
land or I am leaving
out the story all for you

No. 1 GEM CLIPS

100

WILLOW BRAND
"Millions Daily"
OVER 75 YEARS OF
        NOESTING, INC.
BRONX, NY USA

Paper clip the postcard
next to the pomegranate
look out
INKHEAD
beside the drawbridge

Child's asleep after eating
a croissant we sliced lengthwise

filled w/pieces of chocolate
& held in tongs over the burner
to melt the chocolate inside the croissant
then peas for dinner
nothing more

The question is who to be writing this
single moon in the daylight
full above INKHEAD
looks like NAKED, the K
etc.
yesterday
crossed the canal

In another, saw you taking tickets
at the theater—a double
the child said, in accordance with my need
as hearing a sound while dreaming
creates a context for itself inside the dream

For instance stop rustling
the sheets I wish the child would
sleep longer in the morning
& here, that you were
do you
erase the ink if you don't like the word
attach to the paper another

*

"and the berry-black Night"
and the kitchen lit
Chinese for <u>willow</u> & <u>stay</u>
are homophones, the paperclip maker
must have known

Henry says apricots
blossom before plum
& plum comes after cherry
which contradicts Japanese classical poems
because of different varieties

Assayez-vous
says the woman beside me at the Fall Café
surprised in 2009
to pay 1.25 for a large
green tea with ginseng

Mortality comes up in the morning
to be buried next to me
the 4-year-old plans
so if we come back to life
we'll be what we see

Startled by the <u>erhu</u>—
Ode to Joy on the platform—
2 travelers
resume listening

*

Here's a drawing on the F train
of a house with 5 keys
part of the house for Donkey
part for 100 electric guitars
whammy bars, wah wah pedals
& the amp as big as Mars

How much can you see of blossoming
the same time as scattering
the line in the *waka* combines

I was pressing
on a friend's heart in a dream
who sent it, invisible
the body as if
coated with oil
not to say "glistening"

*

The lemon drops taste like pine
as a pine branch would if you put it
in your mouth

Scurvy scurvy-grass in the *waka*
still open on the table
looking closely
back at me?

I am not on fire I am on the fire
escape
sunset at least   out the window

From the Westbeth roof we saw a chair
strapped to a dancer's back
J asked why the dancer's mouth was open—
didn't ask about the chair

Beds sing, he thinks, not mothers
to make a child sleep   he's happy
about that memory
the bridge is singing
(having drawn a bridge he says it sings)
without a camera here's a record
of a week in January

       *

"A Hundred Thousand Shirts," she read aloud, suddenly
Elizabeth Bowen wrote that of Paris
I'm reading Astragali
are numerous out West, the most common genus
of flowering plants
2 can be dissimilar
as a milkweed and a grass

There were objects being named, being lifted
out of the mother's box: a key
paintbrush
stone

& silver
antique nail file
surprisingly hard to explain

Now purposes can be less crossed
The girl was "crossing Paris" when she saw the shirts
not shirts: the sign, not attached
to a surface, just words
floating by, fleet

Half the spider plant seems wilting, so to turn it
toward the sun I turn the table
& the plant moves with it   we are reading
different things, each friend and I
who have four pigs
we eat different amounts of meat, Henry and I
the smallest was Eyelash
the biggest, T. V.

We placed the wooden cardinal next to the collage
of animals rooting in flowers
cut from seed catalogues in tiny squares
& overlappingly pasted, each size a different scale
then vegetables were added
so the pig has a pumpkin on her jowl,
pint of strawberries across her ear

The eggplant are beautiful as in the fields
where men pretend they're penises

hanging out of their zippers
and dance around
don't believe this
moment was repeated
but it happened once

Sky
has a stretch in its action
the lens curves without thinking
may be included the hoop house
gets built in the snow
for early tomatoes called Sun Gold
Elizabeth
put an x there instead, keep going
Elixabeth in several directions

   *

I left my great-grandmother's china out in the yard
a crow swooped down and stole it
or it got washed away
down a cliff the house was perched on
in a big rain doesn't matter
was a dream
also thinking of the soft-mix bread
in a pan left uncovered in the kitchen
sometimes the hens
walked in & sat on it
A raccoon stole a loaf
of other bread cooling on the sill

128

the cat was alive too
birds like
the sun
enough to go to Florida every winter
one just flew at the eave, whole wingspan spread
against the glass

      Ukulele

on a keyboard
everything in blue ink, as an increase
being drawn
a sketch is
something drawn   a curtain
is behind a tree the knight rides toward
(a balance toy beside the cactus)
a list of everything inside the room
or only what can move itself
move <u>by</u> itself
would look like this
cranberry chain on black thread
a draft comes in
things waver
as a thought does & desire
waits for a breeze

That boy lying down with the weight of the ground
pushing back against his weight, did correspond
by breathing—if he thought so then or later

hard to say   you miss me
when I sleep late in the morning

      Milk

       Bread

       Gin

the child writes
his first list
& lines of the letters are odd
on insect legs

(and   )

Bread wanders off into others
possible: Breast
or Break
Be good
to bugs
his t-shirt said
before the letters wore off
strangely
& the child grew
out of clothes
I'm sorry

not to have looked at the book on Joshua's shelf
called *The Spider*, by a spider-
lover
it was difficult
to choose
A Cordiall
Water—didn't finish but I'd like to
hear about your troubles with a muscle
and its cure   the ground
opens rarely
don't be afraid

Also, the king is riding
in a coconut shell on the sill   am not
lying down, not standing up
not even reading "the king is riding"   not rid
of kin—can't keep them
from occurring
        summer-like
a leap year
has how many days? Ten more
than us-
ual   hi Anthony thanks for the honey
you left on the table   a Table
of Circular Measure appears at the back
with Tables of Surface
& Time Measure too
in these speckled, PIED notebooks
the world comes in

the notes go out
& conversely, if you can

We've taken down the winter tree
as Richard said   in Wicker Park
we'll hear John Beer, who knew Cordelia
has new work & I have old
steam heat
a list can change
cranberry jam on black bread, the ear goes along
the night comes on
that star
out there's an airplane
not a broom

    *

Old typo of <u>windrows</u>
can be broken   any spell
we lived in for a while, not liking
to pick the beans

   —would be best to go walking   the clouds are high
higher than the sky with no kites   here, Jane
this is where I am a kite

Brooklyn/Manhattan/Chicago, 2009

VII.

clara luna parce que la jour

that's big, child-face

your nose doubles the sun

Lotus Eaters! go on hoping

one doesn't care for tiny situations

Little Mama poet creates heat

in 10 minutes because u rush-me

wind knits the rest of the letters

to tide's quiet semblance—start again

clear moon because the day

Sort of thinking, of the willows
you can see they like the birch trees and the water
then I don't know what happened.

Seven poplars died of sorrow

A man was too tall for his body

Fixing your eye on the bark to see out to branches beyond, stuff breaks into
straight lines merged with a spectrum of light through the eyelashes. Straight
lines of the spectrum are overlaid by circles, maybe that is the lash curve and
the light looks through you.

Once in a while, being startled

backward, forth, ~~interrupts~~

~~into present~~

interrupts

a future person being only

a space in the cedar grove

~

Can you carry this object
front to back as a room
in a man with straw-
colored hair, I asked
myself and Catherine

answered—she's French I don't know
what she said
the good, tall, looking
guy in the bath wants
music for
it must
be Socratic or else
stanzaic, a part
of the object that carries
itself, but what
is it
asking
listened
Catherine

Oh the kestrel
made no noise

I don't see
I don't know where
The water sounds as
it goes out not only
coming "in."

Get off at 35th
walk up 10th Ave
4 blx
to 34th

7 Station is btwn
10 & 11
take 7 to Grand Central
(or 6 to 33rd)

And the question is, can you help not throw that rock back out the window

The left foot goes down harder, louder.

What is a winter onion?

When you open a letter
a forest appears
yellow & green & gold

A chickadee was upside down
on (under) a crabapple branch, walking along
even while spinning

It was the Sunflower Hotel drifting in
the open window in the storm

Also the correspondence
between Lincoln and Marx

A cinder shape conflicts with dust

Time to drive with caution
over Kelly's Mountain

Secretly saying to my father
Please come back I want to see you again.

Knees untrack, why unto thee intend.

~

Loose-leaf

Dear [   ]   think of
                  person   like x =
                                      y
                  positive
                  or mysterious

You are ____

If you were a food you wd be ____   hypothetical

If you were a city you wd be ____   [not a place]
                                                all 5 vowels
                                                math
                                                a stranger mercy
                                                than the tiger

As for me, I . . .

Lie [   ]
Origin
story

And today I heard . . .

~~And later right now~~
   Anyway, I wish . . .

And right now I can see . . .

October 1, 2017

the hickory is full of
    fruit

It's not a time for

What is it time for

Shut with its rime door

   ~

teaching notes

self assigned to others

   sidereal pulse . . .

What is this book?
Is this the book?

   play "Sun"

~

Worksheet

Fifth day of Spring
2014
is full of snow
like the first, second, and third

An abecedarium

in the snowbook, my notebook mostly blank
I see begins with Ah
                   Bright
                   Cow
                   Doing
                   Everything
                   Fine,
                   Get
                   Happy
                   It
                   Jeers

The abc poem stopping there
gives way to
                   Halves
                   Bell Tree
                   does she talk about how she knows?

I don't know what I meant or thought.

Last year, first week of March was 85 degrees
Now we ski between the rows

An archive selves   a page falls out

Carry the flat star bucket
across the sky field it works better
telescopic / scope to tell of
I did smile ordinary?

Appears I was translating
a thing now missing   sound by sound

Feather falls UP
out of the bed

If you keep looking at <u>snow</u> you'll see the word <u>now</u>

& was the Ice Age woman carved of mammoth tusk not a woman but a sea crea-
ture w/dolphin nose. If you hold the tusk the opposite way, "upside down," that's
what you might see. We don't know how the carver held it, he or she or they.

~

winter and summer

where
inside
night

the
ear
returns

all
new
day

sinking
under
massive
men

~

"When the fog was all gone, Bear felt sad."

When the fog was a noun, Ear left mad.
We were all listening to each other's pencils
in a room with no fog. A cloud had a dog
in its paws, and that made no one sad;
it was the news that stabbed.

Oh, the brightly colored pictures
oh the apple-buttered hand—you got stuck
in a jar of jam.

~

Sundial

& scattered in the sleep past dreamt
am seen in wind   that same again
ExxonMobil
slick spill comes toward
fishes & birds
can be listed
past sleep   & put asunder   in the nesting season

Out the window it looks fine
Yahara River is a river
meeting up with Lake Mendota
men & bicycles   women & boats
hello leigh hunt   and leif and laynie
in a century   with May in it   2010

May not intend it
to be out of joint   earth
under earth
altering
One toad pops up in the shade—fat toad—cools down

yellow and purple   lupine & paintbrush   mt. st. helens
cousin helena   solar nostril for the left breath or vice versa
yvette's mother had a book called *The Sensuous Woman* on licking
we didn't have a lot to say

If A builds a strawbale house it will be round and
Mary & I were fastest in the three-legged race

now move along desire
out of that sound
pattern as   parents as   parts
toward midnight not sleeping   what's that house called in your brain
dial of sun the ground's a bed for
plain way the shadow indicates   calendaric
a present!
from aunt ruth in san francisco   california   why golden
what day

~

The plums kept darkness as a net

those actual trees out back I wish to see
the pattern of a city in some branches, having both
to float the arms up and to sound
a few things out

"For it is not a Description only of Nature, but a Breaking of Nature
into great and strange works"

"We procure means of Seeing Objects a-farr off . . .
and representing things Neare as A-farr off
and things A-farr off as Neare; Making Faigned Distances"

Through the blossoms in a costume
whir the jugglers across the field
seeded down in winter wheat

PROSPEROSA eggplant

FLORIDOR zucchini

MIRABELLE a plum

LANCELOT the leek

Repeating that the world is

"nearest the verge we still thought

ours by right, to break"

~

Yesterday was Wednesday?

All Saints' Day, mother's birthday, Nov. 1?

I don't remember whether it was cold out?

but Michael dug potatoes?

Pianos?

Thursday is goats' milk day but I'm supposed to write about yesterday?

One grows used to the weather?

1 parked car on Evergreen?

The last thing in another thing is The Man Who Planted Trees, underlined, &

two columns keeping score (?)

   The Man Who Planted Trees

H	L
45	~~12~~
~~42~~	
~~36~~	
81	

~

Red start or Fire tail
    makes nest of green moss
    lines it w/wool—lays 9 eggs
    end of April
           p. 140 (Clare natural history prose)

"& sing in one as common as the other" p. 67

"The eye travels along the paths cut out for it in the work" (Klee)

"shorn with a hook instead of being mown with a scythe, & stoukd in shoves like wheat" p. 50

Northborough sonnets p. 4: <u>poetry against itself</u>

About summer come
a trade and a
tradesman
a full day
everyone spoke

& noisome sorrow
hands to mouth
hunger/message
others' edges
will not fit
the trade to shape a Lune
moth

Others could tell the difference
had started lightly to rain
on the top-bar hives
between dream and dream

Last summer: drought
and the hottest July on record.
This summer: the most rain ever recorded
plus some very hot days.

~

"News paper Miracles Wonders Curiousitys &c &c"

What did he say he did with the beeswax? Shot it out of a torch to coat the floor,
and the floor was sealed, gleaming, a fabulous smell. Then a flood came and
lifted the beeswax layer right up, completely off, and the floor is back to sod in
the strawbale house.

In another way she was starting to be able to <u>see</u> the story, its palpable nature,
in addition to what appeared to be happening and what was.

~

    FIRE HORSE SHOWS
    IN THE GIRL WITH THE GIANT BIG TOE

THE RIBCAGE IS A MOBILEthe ribcage is a mobile
ARTICULATE STRUCTUREarticulate structure

~

How Animals Grieve
has an elephant on the cover
a mother elephant no doubt
James said the book
looks interesting or did I

~

November 1st, 2nd, or 3rd

Take a sick day to remember
Mr. Fishman, studying French
in time to be 80 March tenth

     Get skiing
     out in the orchard
     here a bird's drawn
     out of sleep

Spruce staying spruce
Birch becoming birch

It isn't one thing
I'm looking at
I mean it's nothing
made of ink

~

A line through a forest
can follow a coastal line

seven breaths later
startle a bee in the orchard

out of the grape it was startled

before now

Time turns around

   the breadth of a hair

or a bee's leg

now

   ~

I have a Catherine
Wheel that is small
so fits in my hand
written tract spins around
the field in your throat
have you really
mothered a tongue
or anything close
to another can breathe

what the other is thinking
is feeling unlike that
no it is yes
both
worlds want note
books, whis-
key, all
memory found
wanting and
being
geo-
heretical you
see a tree is
missing an arm

~

the beautiful idealism?
    "Idealism"—Berkeley?
Rajan: autometaphoric?

habit of
reading
does not
~~result in~~
reading to see mysteries solved in the moment of reading

~

Unpredicted, snow fell
so the dog ran around and the baby looked around
and we all stayed home from the town.
What a lot of snow does
is keep falling like the same sound
& stars on the ground
(illusion of snow)
under especially streetlights.
Also the branches get soft-looking
& lamps in the windows more gold.
If we saw from the sidewalk
the cat not minding the snow
a rabbit not minding the snow
from under a fir tree
what would it like be
to stand underneath and be home.

~

Language goes on General Strike
one dream says
nothing kept
a poem

~

I observe Kellen walking in the middle of the inner garden. It won't take 45
minutes to write twelve sentences.

I can see, I think, a student's shoe lying on its side in the grass, not on his foot. The skateboarder off to the right is barefoot too.

Someone coughing, and Caryn walking back this way. The orange ball going up and down may be being tossed by Kellen, who may be lying down beside the flowering hedge I think.

~

Writing to see what can remember [of] what was read while slept—not what the sleeper read but [I] but he already having read as marked with corners folded

owls
letters
vowels consonants loved while reading as fore-
told an
hand contained in and combined as both
before and aft in kept [a]
long the casing of my lungs this
arc-shape of a humming
rest
address you always in our

26 bones in each foot
27 in the hand

Head space opens to forest

Don't wear a hat in the woods

~

"Snow taken from the high peaks of mountains might be carried to hot places and let to fall at festivals in open places at summer time." In fact that's the end of the notebook, da Vinci p. 361. No need to fold it over as I first did to find it again. When they freeze on the branch, you can ski out & suck the juice from the insides of apples. I've described this in many ways. The apple body keeps the juice most of the winter; it doesn't matter that the apple's withered. Yellow ones are best for this; ask Henry why. Ashmead's Kernel, Saint Edmund's Pippin. Suma cupped the frozen apples in her mittens one after the other and sucked the ice-cold juice out. It's easy to teach and to do.

~

Carnation in French: œillet, like œil (eye).
The eye [opens] a carnation.

Hidden in the lilacs, the same two girls with a basketball
as were there nine years ago

Matt Baird appeared on the usual bus
both he and I prefer to sit alone but after considering
sat together all four days & had a conversation

~

As I was driving through Dolly's window
stumpaty, stampaty, stomp.

A method is a gimmick very often
said a crow upon a stone. Take pie #347
with ceramic bluebird through which steam comes out.
The edges of its crust are fluted, as a skirt will
ripple in a light wind without music.

~

Smash this

You look smashing
Anarchia
said some weather
we're having, one
after another

What the eye's fixed on
keeps flitting, cat shadow
across the grass
and
extreme
ORANGE
of
SCARLET
Runner
Beans

~

Certain feet are large like boats, Sabine said in her kitchen, looking down at my shoes. Boat with sail, head w/pencils in it, blue elephant, head with pens & pencils in it, bird-head wearing hat, pink and blue rat, small framed photograph, accordion, accordion.

On the sidewalk all contents of a child's toy kitchen had been carefully cleaned and bagged: plates & cups by the dozen, forks, knives, spoons, pretend food from all 4 groups, cans of cola, cocoa, oysters. Toy espresso maker (this was Paris), pots with lids. An entire kitchen with nothing to do. I know, let's bring it home.

I see my glasses out the window on a block of wood from yesterday. In a hurry, we leave the vowels out of words. The glasses are upside down.

She could see through the other voice—birds, horse, voice—when shortly not at all had any of it happened. Whose body made her sleepy was she thinking, in the absence of smokers, missing them.

~

Unicycle song structure
of someone walking
the edge of a mountain
a style of waking, eyes closed
disappears from the text
as snow into snow
to return to the text
a secret comic plot within the audible
sensing it
December begins

~

May 2004–December 2017

The day went by
she said at the end of the day that went by.

The neighbor and the baby and the bees went by
being chased between hemlocks and the garbage
by bees the day went by.

A midwife with her scale and paisley cloth
came to weigh the baby, an event. Event went by.

Seepages between collective and a person's grief
get going like some highway noise. Sunshine,
can you work the remote? Can you be more philosophical
and not adore? There once were many things to say
we said, and waited, and it was this by which the difficult
was made to work. Because you knit the letters
to the leaves around the ladder, there in the sideyard, a surprise.

She says beautiful in the daytime's
the best you can say of the newborn
and the canyon in the Fall.
You have failed me
thirteen years
and one half later, says the poem
to the pan of onions
to the sound of highway traffic.

~

Morning now, afterrain, owe 50
to painter in London
for *Green Engineering Object*
on Wm Morris honeysuckle,
lost-book-cover, *Current* cover
glimpse of lake I caught (caught?)
PERFECT LAUNDRY
block-painted on gray brick
Most Garments $2.50 and
LUU'S BODY
is LUU'S **AUTO**BODY
on closer look

2 birds fly the wrong way unless I'm on the wrong train—TONS of pigeons all at
once just now flew off a rooftop, landing all together on cement where crumbs or
something dead is spread. Christmas Trees already in the Ace lot—it's Sep-
tember 23rd—stayed home last night & wrote about the Equinox.

I'd like to feel a difference in my body when the Earth is different in its space
that moment very early in the morning

~

Everything's under the trainwhistle, jackhammer, exhalation
of the kneeling bus   later in summer
100 frogs

Yes we ate no beef or game, just glided by the bees and the males, who admired our *qi* and our paisley tie.

~

    No form
of memory imagined that
natatoriums at night are hard to find
but ripply and if
glass-roofed, star-topped.
Specific numbers of muscles
involve a person's
form of wishing, still to think
some time inventive of itself
and in attendance
of the spherical leaves
of the olive tree, a wind is
present, forming.

~

Not making the bed not
threading ragweed or those
scruffy miniature daisies in
the bike chain, not reading
Nin, just Clover in the
Guardian, not waking up
with ~~lines~~
words in my head,

rather with a cat on my
head, having also
been waked by the cat's cry
earlier across the room & having
mistaken that cry for "Mama," having then waked up the baby
thinking the baby awake & crying
and a few years later 13
and a half to be
exact, I find the next page
doesn't say what happened or
what didn't happen next
instead I find

"Experience, already reduced to a swarm of impressions, is ringed round for
each one of us by that thick wall of personality through which no real voice has
ever pierced on its way to us, or from us to that which we can only conjecture to
be without"

       —probably Pater but doesn't the syntax do something weird; is the
voice <u>to</u> or <u>from</u>, is he changing his mind in the middle

    ~

Also the daily tumble
of the oversized bear, head over paws
all the way down
to a seated position
are you still
not sure how it goes

VIII.

process
walking
notebook
birds' nests & toads
500 for 12 hours
poetry
prose
growing over

~

steering-wheel-in-the-field
is an imaginary flower
on the bent-down path
of foxtail and weeds
joyous to find a rusted-out car there
i was 14

~

We looked for rocks
in Main-à-Dieu.
One was a seal

or a fish
a bird
in the kitchen now
over the sink.
Particular lines
in stones are <u>veins</u>
& you haven't stuck to the fact
that <u>now</u>
is a redundant word

~

Alphabet in Oklahoma

Animal bodies aren't different from plant, planet, actual
bodies:
cicadas, terra
dactyls
elephants, eggplant, mother elephants
fools
giant boulders
husks of barley—<u>husk</u> from ME *huske*, from OE *husuc, hosuc* ("little covering,
    sheath"); the outer membranous or green envelope of some fruits or seeds, as
    that of a walnut or an ear [of corn]—from Low German *hüske* ("little house,
    sheath"), see Dutch *huysken,* diminutive of *hus* ("house"); plural <u>husks</u>
inchworms and mint-
julep colored Glassy-Winged Toothpick Grasshoppers, Splendid Tiger Beetles,
    Papago Thread-Legged Katydids, Half-Moon male Betta Fish . . . for <u>moon</u> I
    first typed <u>noon</u>, perhaps because *Chronos* and

Kairos I
learned as one kind of time and other kind of time. Also,
maybe you
notice how screech
owls,
purple martins, each tree growing in a
quincunx,
radish, rye and all
such minerals as Selenite
tell of day and night and
weather—oops a <u>u</u> and <u>v</u> come first, so
unto self say nothing, nothing is
vanity, or
why must it all be—
eXamine the evidence, earthling, and see what
you think the letter
<u>Z</u> could begin.

~

James goes to school, assigned to write
a paper on Canadian Geese:
The Canada Goose Problem.
Gets help from Chuck Stebelton
all day walking, watching.
Concludes Canadian Geese are not a problem.
Says there's a human problem.

~

Another OK ABC, Great Salt Plains State Park
for Lewis Freedman and Richard Meier

Animal plant & mineral
bodies aren't different from WORD BODIES, a Selenite
Crystal might tell you if you
dug it out by hand & shovel, not really dug but LOOSENED OUT with water
    that you carried to the hole you dug, then poured water carefully around as
    soon as any crystal-bit appeared and let the rest of it
emerge, just as every space between each word and every space between each
    letter (such as between the e and
f in effluence)
gets going, gets alive, but
how?
It was going to start backward, this
jostled alphabet continuing a
kinescopic way of seeing from behind or
like the snake with its tail in its mouth, which isn't
much of a beginning but may sort of
name an intervolving shape, an
overlapping idea of
progression—poor snake or knowing snake, poor knowing snake, infinitely self-
    conjoined. I had a student named
Quiamah and I'd
rather write her name for q than find a word I haven't used in *Webster's*
Seventh though I found an insect called

Timema californicum when looking for a pict-
ure of a certain
verdant color, mint-julep, to be
whistle-clear
x-act. And was surprised by *californicum*, the word, as ever-
y (ever-y) word & letter are surprised, I mean alive akin to plants & animals &
    everything as stated here, beginning over with both
z and a

~

Oil the breadboards and don't remember
to forget a story you almost told
of hunters in Ostuni shooting birds
over the child's head (shot fluttered down)
as he was carried on Henry's shoulders
through olive groves in January

How does it go, the rest of the story
must've been in a hurry

the day before a birthday
a red pine is all arms
you can reach toward, enter and climb
in the spiral too

~

Pedagogical Sketchbook, p. 47:

 EARTH, WATER AND AIR.

Symbols of the static area are plummet (position) and balance.
The plummet aims at the earth center where all materially-bound
existence is anchored.

But there are regions with different laws and new symbols, signifying
freer movement and dynamic position.

Water and atmosphere are transitional regions.

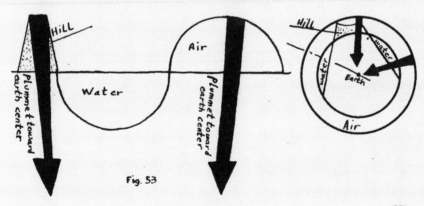

Fig. 53

47

~

Page from a book on astronomy

Seven persons in the buckwheat

Spies in the book taking notes

   about the Driftless
region of Wisconsin
where the glaciers never were
& i live near

   (Blue Mounds, Viroqua, Black Earth . . .)

It's Spring and usually it's Fall,
Canadian father born at midnight
in Montréal Japan

The first plum tree's in blossom
what kind of plum tree ask Henry
if there's a ghost in my hair

After the rain there were 23 more
shiitake than the day before
thanks to the oak that fell
& Skinny Pete the mushroom
midwife

I'd rather sleep than plant potatoes
and the onions don't mind waiting
that's how they grow
not grow so much as form
around their selves inside the ground
Notice when you're peeling one that this is so

then there was writing you couldn't read
inside the trees and the stones
on hair's-breadth stems & chickens' claws
& pads of the dog's feet between each nail
where she loves to have pressure, where all her nerves
come to an end, or start, like our own

    Intelligent nerve endings
where the experiment begins

      *

Monocrops go by the windows
of the bus I'm lying down in like an onion

Spring buds, light green at the ends of branches
where the writing went walking

"Off into the raptures," Joanne said
so
an elegy appears
because I miss her,
didn't know her

About here she'd notice something
most likely alive or attached to
someone alive, like his hat
(Philip Whalen's) or a mouse
or a bird, many birds
[name some from her poems]
FISHER NUTS
(I've just looked up)
FISHMAN WRITES
on the bus to Chicago
for Joanne Kyger

                —April 18, 2017

            ~

Discerned

checking on mushrooms—Golden
Oyster growing on mulberry
Shiitake on red oak and
other kinds of oyster—Gray Dove
        Blue Dolphin etc on box
                            elder
Before getting there past
the second rise
to the edge of the woods
what I discerned
before the second rise

I saw that
melons ripen by sleeping in
the sun
they get fat in the sun
                    sweetening
up
    pressing in
to the ground

every day they get more sleep
and every night too under
        the ~~small bright~~ moon
            bright small

Like a melon in July
I slept and slept

breath't and breath't

   ~

Over 35
varieties today
Adam's Pearmain
Ashmead's Kernel
Cox's Orange Pippin
Cornish Gillyflower
Karmijn de Sonneville
Roxbury Russet

Foxwhelp
Wolf River
Calville Blanc d'Hiver
Blue Pearmain
are some of them.

~

A nuthatch walked up the box elder
seems more than can be said

~

crankshaft pulley
dropped on the ground &
we will need a tow
dirty honey
is the poem

~

bpN says "they covered each other with longing"
he says it in different ways
"i place my longing in my voice & say hello"
"i place my longing in my eyes & see her"
"we looked into each others faces & saw the longing there"
"the longing flowed out of me into her fingertips"
"we covered each other with longing"
—not in that order and with many other things

but i think he'd be ok with this
Nights on Prose Mountain is on my knees
he was alive   i ask him if
they left each other
free of longing
they had never been together   so they didn't leave
then again, i change a word, i offer him
"<u>uncovered</u> with longing"

~

my name is lisa fiction   when i read fiction
am a fishmanal character   i've been told

~

Spoon Fest

      drifty
   river in the Driftless
   love you I
have a birch spoon
      supple, said someone
      for carving
  Shapely, the mind is
for making
      shape-ily, maybe
      notice

    elaborate caterpillar
   on the brick wall
    flowing <u>up</u>, not inching along

  *

Medium current yesterday, faster thru the culverts with no boats
under the bridge under the highway
       County P off 131
      between Viroqua & La Farge

Hey James I said to his bobbing head, we got here before the glaciers

  *

Next day
under a long-voweled tree
(maple)
start with a blank
a block of wood
to which you take the axe.
Short-voweled trees
softer for knife-work
are bass, aspen, birch.

What got carved:
a buckthorn spoon
"   " masher
hawthorn spreader (for butter)

~~scrappy wood spatula~~ a bird
or 2-handled thing
not changing the wood
        into paper or copper

   ~

Postcard from Montréal
    written on Rock Island, Wisconsin

What do you think about
spiders' eyes Tara looks at
with a headlamp
as she walks down a
path. Says she can discern
the glistening in
grasses & brambles
        and each
time she is correct: a spider
in a leaf or branch.
Henry tried it and
saw only dew.
I tried and
saw only grasses & brambles,
leaves & branches.
An elm sleep makes its way
thru my body under the
elm trees in the elm
grove

where vowels are long to
join
& made me up
to dream it then I woke
and bit my tongue

Vowel head you are a dandelion's
seed-part left to blow and wish,
not the yellow flower testing
love of butter such as if
the chin turns yellow when it's pressed
there is no other lover than the plover
says the solitary rhyme
which found its
walking thru a
field of glossy three-leaved
plants, this poison ivy meadow
in an elm grove
What kind of animal are you?
Two are digging a hole
twice the size of
they themselves
they disappear in it
the sand flies up
they're digging with their hands
Are you getting to know dog nature
they shake their heads no—I'm tired of jam
showing up in poems every summer
so won't make any
until next year

Tara was looking at tadpoles
I joined her &
looked, to be polite
then got interested
bc a few had front legs but most had only
back legs
which clearly develop first
and when they get their
front legs they look like
frogs
which they're becoming

I will look at them every day
Tara says, to see how
long it takes
to become a frog

We've never seen a bean
or a wolf
except in a zoo
bean should be bear if typed
but today we saw a snake

The sun enclosed in the
meadow it appears, but is not
so I will walk across
the poison ivy field if it
is a p.i. field   time will tell
and leave the grass bed for a

in an elm grove
for cedar trees
around
and so
& also having just been
stung by a thing
I didn't see at all
on upper right thigh
not bad but probably a bee
well there are the late
summer lions—the kind the light shows in
their fuzzy silky transparent circular
mobile seed-fluff heads
the wind blows through
but not off

Acknowledgments

In addition to the editors who published portions of this book in magazines or anthologies cited below, I thank Brian Teare for publishing *At the same time as scattering* as a chapbook (Albion Books, San Francisco, 2010); Jordan Dunn for producing *Deer 1* as a pamphlet and the Oklahoma ABC poems as a broadside on Oxeye Press (Des Moines, 2015 and 2018); Dawn Pendergast for producing "Can you carry this object" as a paper airplane for the Ephemera Issue of *Little Red Leaves* (Chicago, 2011); and Laynie Browne for including a portion of "November 16–December 1, 2016" in the Women's March Solidarity Texts (2017). The latter poem in full is indebted procedurally to Matvei Yankelevich's *The Nature of Poetry of Matvei Yankelevich* (Ugly Duckling Presse, 2011). For certain shared writing practices, deep and ongoing thanks to Lewis Freedman, Amy Lipman, Abigail Zimmer, and many students at Columbia College Chicago.

Portions of this book were first published in the journals gratefully acknowledged here: *American Letters & Commentary, Aurochs, Black Clock, Chicago Review, Columbia Poetry Review, Court Green, Denver Quarterly, ecopoetics, Evening Will Come (The Volta), Jacket2, Laurel Review, Mary, Milwaukee Journal-Sentinel Express, MiPOesias, Parthenon West Review, 6x6, SplitLevel Journal*. "As I was driving through Dolly's window" was published as "Evening Without Swallows" in *Not for Mothers Only: Contemporary Poems on Child-Getting & Child-Rearing* (Fence Books, 2007); "steering-wheel-in-the-field" is anthologized in *The Arcadia Project: North American Postmodern Pastoral* (Ahsahta Press, 2012) and in *Ecopoetics* (Trinity University Press, 2013); "The plums kept darkness as a net" was a Rabbit Light Movie (2008); and prose from "On the Beara Peninsula" was part of the Starkweather Arts Center exhibit of paintings by Barbara Driscoll Clay (2018).

Finally and always, I'm deeply grateful to the following people: Henry James Morren, James Fishman-Morren, Richard Meier, Joshua Beckman, Lotte Langer, Brenda Hillman, and Michael Palmer. My thanks also to Young Shakespeare Players, Driftless Folk School, and Friends of Lorine Niedecker. The final(?) shape/s of this book were found on Cape Breton Island, Nova Scotia. I thank Sean Howard, Lee-Anne Broadhead, and Anita Lahey of Main-à-Dieu for helping that happen.

Images from Paul Klee's *Pedagogical Sketchbook*, translated by Sibyl Moholy-Nagy, are used with permission from Copyright Clearance Center. Quoted and paraphrased da Vinci material is from *The Notebooks of Leonardo da Vinci, Compiled and Edited from the Original Manuscripts by Jean Paul Richter* (Dover Publications, two volumes).